Cheetahs, the Swift Hunters

by GLADYS CONKLIN

pictures by CHARLES ROBINSON

HOLIDAY HOUSE · New York

For MARION GARTHWAITE,
a jolly companion on
many "book" adventures

Text copyright © 1976 by Gladys Conklin
Illustrations copyright © 1976 by Charles Robinson
All rights reserved
Printed in the United States of America

Library of Congress Cataloging in Publication Data

Conklin, Gladys Plemon.
    Cheetahs, the swift hunters.

    SUMMARY: Describes the life style of a mother
cheetah and her cubs during their first eighteen months.

    1. Cheetahs—Juvenile literature. [1. Cheetahs]
I. Robinson, Charles, 1931-   II. Title.
QL737.C23C65   599´.74428   76-6446
ISBN 0-8234-0280-0

Author's Note

The cheetah is an unusual animal in many ways. It has rare beauty and surprising gentleness for a predator. Perhaps the most unexpected thing is its voice. It has no growl or roar like the lion, only a birdlike chirp. The unusual trait that is the cheetah's alone is its speed.

The cheetah is a sprinter, not a racer. With its small round head, deep chest, and long legs, it is well adapted for speed. The average cheetah weighs between 120 and 140 pounds, and is seven feet long from its nose to the tip of its tail.

They are solitary animals. They don't live in groups except for the mother and her cubs. If a cheetah is crossing a field and sees another approaching, it will turn aside and look the other way.

We are indebted to Randall L. Eaton for his study of the wild cheetah. He went to East Africa in 1966 and has written his first book, *The Cheetah: The Biology, Ecology, and Behavior of an Endangered Species.*

We need to know more about this impressive animal that is being rapidly destroyed. The ancient Egyptians hunted with the cheetah; Marco Polo described them in the court of Kubla Khan.

Are we going to let the cheetah disappear from the earth?

The early morning sun cast a warm glow over the Serengeti Plains of East Africa. On the top of the small mound of a termite nest sat a lone female cheetah. Her golden fur and amber eyes reflected the glow of the sun. The cubs that she had cared for over the past eighteen months had left her. They had learned to chase and to catch and to kill. They no longer needed their mother.

The lonely cheetah was restless. A strong mating urge was driving her to look for a mate. She was watching a golden head coming closer and closer through the tall dry grass. A handsome male cheetah stopped a few paces from her. They stared hard at each other. All at once the female rose to her feet. The male turned and ran. The female accepted his invitation to a mating chase.

The cheetahs chased each other in and out of the bushes for two days. They would lie down and groom each other and spend long minutes licking each other's faces. Soft sounds and murmurs came from the bushes. The chase ended when the female moved over on her belly and allowed the male to mount her.

For the next three months the female cheetah lived alone. She continued to sit on a termite mound, from which she watched for small antelopes. While her cubs were developing inside her, she needed to hunt for food every day. One morning she felt life stirring actively in her body. She looked for a thick thorn bush where she could hide her cubs.

The next morning there were three small blind cubs squirming around close to their mother. Her long pink tongue worked busily, licking and cleaning each wet body. As each cub's face dried, the "beauty mark" of the cheetah stood out clearly—a bold black stripe like a tear-stain running from the inner corner of each eye to the corner of the mouth.

The cubs were born with a covering of long hair shimmering across their shoulders and down their backs. This protects them from the rain and hot sun. It gradually wears off during the third month.
The newborn cubs had faint spots showing on their legs and bodies. Halfway down their tails the spots changed to black bands, with a white tuft on the end.

The mother stretched out to let the cubs nurse. She
purred contentedly as they pressed their faces
against her belly. They nursed and slept and
wakened to nurse again. When they couldn't feel
their mother, they made thin chirping sounds almost
like the chirp of a bird. The mother also chirped.
She had no roar like the lion.

The cheetah moved her new cubs many times
during the first few weeks. She moved one at a
time, picking up each twelve ounces of warm
softness gently by the back. If a lion roared nearby,
she moved them at once to a new hiding place.
If she saw a hyena snooping around in the bushes,
she moved them again. In spite of her care, one cub
was killed.

Early one morning when the cubs were six weeks
old, their mother led the remaining two out of the
bushes. She took them to the top of a low termite
hill. From now on they would go with her every day.

The cubs sat close to their mother on the mound.
Their eyes were big with curiosity as they looked out
across the plains. A field of animals stretched on
and on as far as they could see.

    They were watching a dust cloud that billowed up
from the flying heels of a small herd of wildebeests
and zebras. Something had disturbed the racing
animals. Blindly following the leader, all were caught
up in the excitement that spread from rushing body
to body.

The mother cheetah's eyes were fixed steadily on a small group of Thomson's gazelles that were grazing by themselves. She was choosing her special prey. For five minutes she watched a small fawn on the edge of the group. She would try to catch this one and no other.

With a warning sound of "ughh" to her cubs to sit and watch, the cheetah walked slowly toward the antelopes. She held her head and body low as she kept her eyes on her intended victim. When the fawn raised its head, the cheetah froze in her tracks. She never moved until the fawn continued feeding.

This slow stop-and-go continued for nearly a half hour. The cheetah had to choose the final moment carefully. She had to be close enough to catch her prey within twenty seconds. She had tremendous speed but she tired quickly.

She moved closer and closer. She finally stopped
and waited tensely, one minute, two minutes. She
needed a one-second head start for success. The
fawn lowered its head and she was ready. She burst
into action. In two great bounds her long legs
carried her into top speed at sixty miles an hour.

The startled fawn leaped wildly into the air and zigzagged across the field. The cheetah followed the sharp turns exactly and in a few seconds was running beside it. One sweep of her big paw across the hind legs and the fawn crashed to the ground. The cheetah seized the warm throat and held on until the animal suffocated.

A shrill chirp from their mother brought the cubs
running. They tugged impatiently at the warm body
as their mother dragged it into the shade of a bush.
For ten minutes she sat panting like a dog after a
hard run.

The cubs were still trying to break through the tough hide when their mother came to help them. She broke the skin and pulled it away from the red meat. The cubs ate greedily until their bellies were as tight as blown-up balloons.

The cheetah was nervous and ate rapidly. She tore huge chunks of meat from the body and gulped them down. She stopped often to look around. Already the big black wings of a vulture had appeared in the sky. Soon others would come, and then the lions would follow.

She quickly urged the cubs away from the meat. When she felt that they had gone far enough, she pushed them into the center of a thick cluster of thorn bushes. She licked each blood-smeared face until it was clean. The cubs cuddled close to the warm fur of their mother and purred as they went to sleep.

During the third month the cubs started learning
how to chase. They stayed close behind their
mother, sniffing each rock and tree and termite hill.
When she froze in her tracks, they instantly froze
beside her. Their ears perked up as they moved
slowly toward a group of grazing antelopes.

They followed at a distance behind her as she dashed in for the kill. As her heavy paw knocked the small gazelle down, the cubs broke into full speed to join her. They couldn't wait but tore at the warm animal while its legs were still twitching.

At five months, the cubs were growing rapidly. Their
bodies were now clearly dotted with strong black spots.
Their stubby baby-legs were growing long and slender.
One morning a young warthog came trotting
through the bushes, its little black tail held stiffly in
the air. The mother cheetah held back and let her
cubs make the chase.

They took off eagerly and knocked the warthog down. But they couldn't hold it or kill it. It was on its feet and running before they knew what was happening. Again they chased and caught it. A swipe of a cub's big paw knocked it to the ground, but it was the mother that rushed up and bit it on the back of the neck.

The cubs spent many hours playing. They chased each other around and around a tree. One would try to climb the tree, the other would pull its tail. They pounced on each other and rolled together in a big furry ball. When they quieted down, they licked each other's faces.

At eighteen months the cubs had their first real success in hunting. Late one afternoon a small herd of antelopes came toward the termite mound. The mother watched quietly but the cubs were very excited. A small fawn was limping along at the rear of the herd. The cubs started walking slowly toward it.

Their excitement grew and they burst into high speed. As they ran beside the fawn, a big paw easily knocked it to the ground. One cub grabbed its throat and held on until the body went limp. Without waiting for their mother, they settled down to feast on their first kill.

During the night the cubs wandered off by
themselves, never to return. They would soon
separate, each to go his solitary way.
The morning sun found the mother cheetah alone
once more. All day she sat on the termite hill
looking out over the grassland. Near twilight she saw
a golden head moving through the grass. She
watched intently for a few minutes, then slowly
walked forward to meet her new mate.